JANICE VANCLEAVE'S
WILD, WACKY, AND WEIRD
SCIENCE EXPERIMENTS

EVEN MORE OF JANICE VANCLEAVE'S
WILD, WACKY, AND WEIRD

CHEMISTRY EXPERIMENTS

Illustrations by
Jim Carroll

New York

This edition published in 2018 by
The Rosen Publishing Group, Inc.
29 East 21st Street
New York, NY 10010

Library of Congress Cataloging-in-Publication Data

Names: VanCleave, Janice Pratt.
Title: Even more of Janice VanCleave's wild, wacky, and weird chemistry experiments / Janice VanCleave.
Other titles: Janice VanCleave's wild, wacky, and weird chemistry experiments | Wild, wacky, and weird chemistry experiments
Description: New York : Rosen Publishing, 2018. | Series: Janice VanCleave's wild, wacky, and weird science experiments | Audience: Grades 5–8. | Includes bibliographical references and index.
Identifiers: LCCN 2016053802| ISBN 9781499466935 (pbk. book) | ISBN 9781508175964 (6 pack) | ISBN 9781499466881 (library bound book)
Subjects: LCSH: Chemistry—Experiments—Juvenile literature.
Classification: LCC QD43 .V356 2018 | DDC 540.78—dc23
LC record available at https://lccn.loc.gov/2016053802

Manufactured in China

Illustrations by Jim Carroll

Experiments first published in *Janice VanCleave's 200 Gooey, Slippery, Slimy, Weird and Fun Experiments* by John Wiley & Sons, Inc. copyright © 1992 Janice VanCleave

CONTENTS

INTRODUCTION

Chemistry is the study of the way materials are put together and their behavior under different conditions. Matter makes up everything in the universe. Chemists study all this matter to learn what it is made of and how it reacts.

The people who decide to work in the field of chemistry have a variety of careers to choose from. Food chemists study the ingredients in what we eat, doctors study biochemistry and the reactions that take place in the body, and forensic chemists work with crime scene evidence. All of these people have something in common: they are constantly asking questions to learn even more about chemistry.

This book is a collection of science experiments about chemistry. What are the attractive forces between water molecules? Can air be cleaned by chemistry? How can you separate the colors in ink? You will find the answers to these and many other questions by doing the experiments in this book.

HOW TO USE THIS BOOK

You will be rewarded with successful experiments if you read each experiment carefully, follow the steps in order, and do not substitute materials. The following sections are included for all the experiments.

» **PURPOSE:** *The basic goals for the experiment.*

» **MATERIALS:** *A list of supplies you will need.* You will experience less frustration and more fun if you gather all the necessary materials for the experiments before you begin. You lose your train of thought when you have to stop and search for supplies.

» **PROCEDURE:** *Step-by-step instructions on how to perform the experiment.* Follow each step very carefully, never skip steps, and do not add your own. Safety is of the utmost importance, and by reading the experiment before starting, then following the instructions exactly, you can feel confident that no unexpected results will occur. Ask an adult to help you when you are working with anything sharp or hot. If adult supervision is required, it will be noted in the experiment.

» **RESULTS:** *An explanation stating exactly what is expected to happen.* This is an immediate learning tool. If the expected results are achieved, you will know that you did the experiment correctly. If your results are not the same as described in the experiment, carefully read the instructions and start over from the first step.

» **WHY?** *An explanation of why the results were achieved.*

Introduction

The Scientific Method

Scientists identify a problem or observe an event. Then they seek solutions or explanations through research and experimentation. By doing the experiments in this book, you will learn to follow experimental steps and make observations. You will also learn many scientific principles that have to do with chemistry.

In the process, the things you see or learn may lead you to new questions. For example, perhaps you have completed the experiment that studies how to blow soap bubbles. Now you wonder how the brand of soap you use affects the size of the bubbles. That's great! All scientists are curious and ask new questions about what they learn. When you design a new experiment, it is a good idea to follow the scientific method.

1. Ask a question.

2. Do some research about your question. What do you already know?

3. Come up with a hypothesis, or a possible answer to your question.

4. Design an experiment to test your hypothesis. Make sure the experiment is repeatable.

5. Collect the data and make observations.

6. Analyze your results.

7. Reach a conclusion. Did your results support your hypothesis?

Many times the experiment leads to more questions and a new experiment.

Always remember that when devising your own science experiment, have a knowledgeable adult review it with you before trying it out. Ask them to supervise it as well.

FLOATING STICKS

PURPOSE To observe the pulling power of water molecules.

MATERIALS 3 toothpicks quart (liter)
glass bowl
liquid dish soap

PROCEDURE

1. Fill the bowl three-quarters full with water.

2. Place two toothpicks side by side on the surface in the center of the water.

3. Treat the third toothpick by dipping its point in liquid detergent. *Note:* Only a very small amount of detergent is needed.

4. Touch the treated toothpick tip between the floating sticks.

RESULTS The sticks quickly move away from each other.

WHY? The surface of water acts as if a thin skin were stretched across it. This allows objects to float on top. Detergent breaks the attraction between the molecules where it touches, causing the water molecules to move outward and taking the floating sticks with them. This outward movement occurs because the water molecules are pulling on each other. It is almost as if the molecules were all playing tug of war, and any break causes the "tuggers" to fall backward.

8

Floating Sticks

MOVING DROP

PURPOSE To demonstrate the attractive force between water molecules.

MATERIALS 1-foot (30-cm) sheet of wax paper
toothpick
eyedropper
water

PROCEDURE

1. Spread the wax paper on a table.

2. Use the eyedropper to position three or four separate small drops of water on the paper.

3. Wet the toothpick with water.

4. Bring the tip of the wet pick near, but not touching, one of the water drops. Repeat with the other drops.

RESULTS The drop moves toward the toothpick.

WHY? Water molecules have an attraction for each other. This attraction is strong enough to cause the water drop to move toward the water on the toothpick. The attraction of the water molecules for each other is due to the fact that each molecule has a positive and a negative side. The positive side of one molecule attracts the negative side of another molecule.

SOAP BUBBLES

PURPOSE To make a soap bubble solution and to blow soap bubbles.

MATERIALS liquid dish soap
cup (250 ml)
8-in (20-cm) piece of 20-gauge wire; any thin
bendable wire will work

PROCEDURE

1. Fill the cup halfway with the dish soap.

2. Add enough water to fill the cup. Stir.

3. Make a 2-in (5-cm) diameter loop in one end of the wire.

4. Dip the loop into the soap solution.

5. Hold the loop, with the thin layer of soap stretched across it, about four inches from your mouth.

6. Gently blow through the film of soap.

RESULTS Bubbles of soap should be produced. If the soap film breaks, try blowing more gently. Add 1 tablespoon (15 ml) of soap to the solution if the bubbles continue to break. More soap should be added until bubbles are produced.

WHY? The soap and water molecules link together to form a zig-zag pattern. This irregular pattern allows the thin layer of liquid to stretch outward when blown into.

FOAMY SODA

PURPOSE To observe gas bubbles being pushed out of a soda by particles of salt.

MATERIALS small baby-food jar
soda, any flavor carbonated beverage
1 tsp (5 ml) table salt

PROCEDURE

1. Fill the jar halfway with the soda.

2. Add 1 teaspoon (5 ml) of salt to the soda.

RESULTS Bubbles form in the liquid, then foam appears on top of the soda.

WHY? Each bubble seen in the soda is a collection of carbon dioxide gas. Salt and carbon dioxide are both examples of matter and matter takes up space. When the salt is added to the cola, bubbles of carbon dioxide stick to the grains. Larger bubbles form and rise to the top, bringing small amounts of soda with them. This movement of the gas forms the foam on top of the liquid, and the process is called effervescence.

Foamy Soda

ERUPTING VOLCANO

PURPOSE To simulate a volcanic eruption.

MATERIALS soda bottle
baking pan
dirt
1 tbsp (15 ml) baking soda
1 cup (250 ml) vinegar
red food coloring

PROCEDURE

1. Place the soda bottle in the pan.

2. Shape moist dirt around the bottle to form a mountain. Do not cover the bottle's mouth and do not get dirt inside the bottle.

3. Pour 1 tablespoon (15 ml) of baking soda into the bottle.

4. Color 1 cup (250 ml) of vinegar with the red food coloring, and pour the liquid into the bottle.

RESULTS Red foam sprays out the top and down the mountain of dirt.

WHY? The baking soda reacts with the vinegar to produce carbon dioxide gas. The gas builds up enough pressure to force the liquid out of the top of the bottle. The mixture of the gas and the liquid produces the foam.

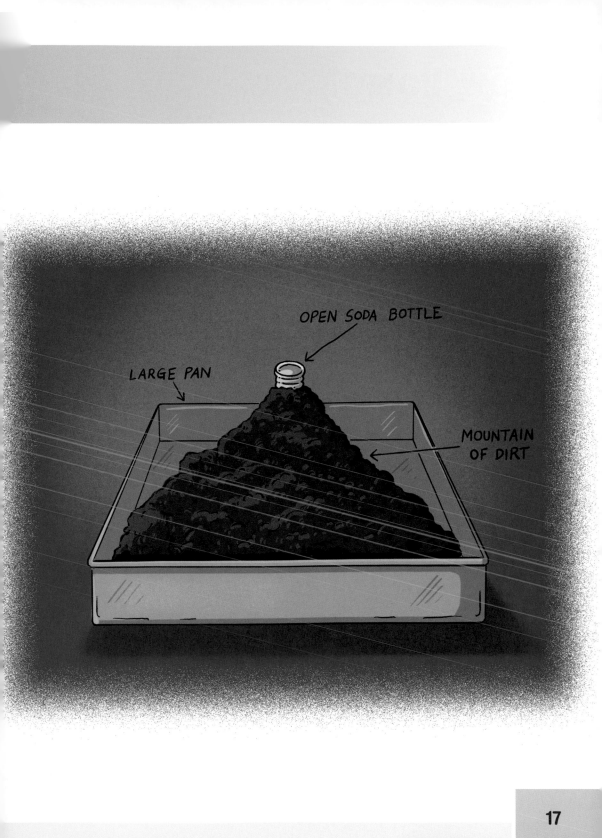

Erupting Volcano

How Long?

PURPOSE To time the release of bubbles produced by one Alka-Seltzer tablet.

MATERIALS soda bottle
measuring cup (250 ml)
clay ball, the size of a walnut
18-in (45-cm) piece of aquarium tubing
1 Alka-Seltzer tablet

PROCEDURE

1. Pour ¼ cup (60 ml) of water into the soda bottle.

2. Squeeze the clay around the tubing about 2 in (5 cm) from one end.

3. Fill the jar with water.

4. Place the free end of the tube in the jar of water.

5. Break the Alka-Seltzer tablet into small pieces; quickly drop the pieces into the soda bottle.

6. Immediately insert the tube into the bottle; seal the opening with the clay.

7. Record the time.

8. Watch and record the time when the bubbling stops.

RESULTS The tablet immediately reacts with the water to produce bubbles. The bubbles are released for about twenty-five minutes.

WHY? The dry acid and baking soda in the tablet are able to combine with the water to form carbon dioxide gas. It is the carbon dioxide gas that moves through the tube and forms bubbles in the glass of water. The bubbling stops when all the material has reacted.

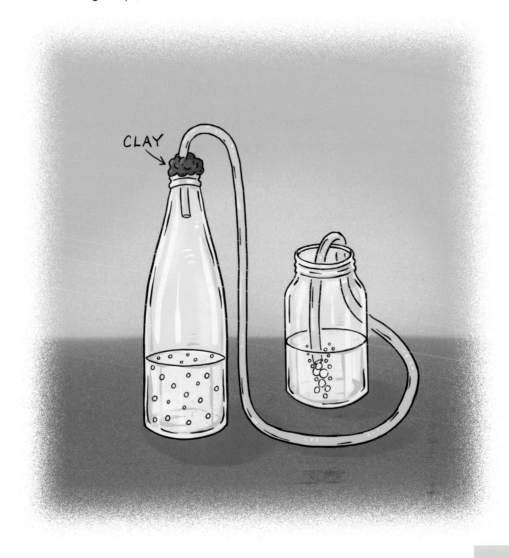

CLAY

BROWNING APPLE

PURPOSE An investigation of the effect that oxygen has on the darkening of fruit.

MATERIALS apple
vitamin C tablet

PROCEDURE

1. Ask an adult to cut the unpeeled apple in half.

2. Crush the vitamin C tablet and sprinkle the powder over the cut surface of one of the apple halves.

3. Allow both apple sections to sit uncovered for one hour.

4. Observe the color of each section.

RESULTS The untreated section turns brown, but the section treated with vitamin C is unchanged.

WHY? Apples and other fruit, such as pears and bananas, discolor when bruised or peeled and exposed to air. This discoloration is caused by chemicals called enzymes. The enzymes are released by the damaged cells and react with oxygen to digest the cells of the fruit. Rapid color and taste changes occur because of the reaction with oxygen. Vitamin C prevents the darkening by reacting with the enzyme before it can start digesting the cell tissue.

AGING PAPER

PURPOSE To observe the rapid aging of a newspaper.

MATERIALS newspaper
automobile

PROCEDURE

1. Lay a piece of newspaper in an automobile so that the sun's rays hit it.

2. Leave the paper in the car for five days.

RESULTS The newspaper appears to have rapidly aged. It changes from white to yellow in color.

WHY? This reaction is unique because it is the reverse of most reactions with oxygen. Usually the addition of oxygen causes the color to become lighter. The materials used to make the newspaper are yellow in color. The chemicals added to turn the paper white do so by removing oxygen. Placing the paper in the car allows the sunlight to heat up the air and the paper, causing oxygen to combine with the chemicals in the paper. The addition of the oxygen changes the paper back to its original yellow color. All newspaper will turn yellow after a period of time. The sun's light just speeded up the aging process.

Aging Paper

Stick On

PURPOSE To demonstrate how air is cleaned by adsorbent chemicals.

MATERIALS
1 cup (250 ml) baking soda
shoe box with a lid
measuring tablespoon (15 ml)
2 pint-size resealable plastic bags

marking pen
adult helper
1 onion
saucer

PROCEDURE

1. Pour 1 cup (250 ml) of baking soda into a shoe box.

2. Remove one tablespoon (15 ml) of baking soda from the box and place it in a resealable plastic bag. With the marking pen, label the bag "UNUSED."

3. Evenly spread the rest of baking soda over the bottom of the box.

4. Ask an adult helper to peel an onion and cut it into four parts.

5. Place the pieces of onion in a saucer.

6. Set the saucer of onions inside the shoe box.

7. Place the lid on the box.

8. After twenty-four hours, remove a tablespoon (15 ml) of the baking soda and place it in a resealable plastic bag. Label the bag "USED."

9. Open the bags one at a time and smell the contents.

RESULTS The contents of the bag marked "USED" smell like an onion.

WHY? Baking soda is adsorbent (other chemicals stick to its surface). Being adsorbent is different from being absorbent. A sponge absorbs or picks up water by taking the water into the material of the sponge. When the baking soda adsorbs the gases given off by the cut onion, the gas molecules stick to the surface of the baking soda. The more the baking soda is spread out, the greater is its surface area and the more adsorbing it is. Baking soda is often placed inside refrigerators to adsorb odors.

CLOSED SHOE BOX

ONION WEDGES

BAKING SODA

USED

UNUSED

RESEALABLE PLASTIC BAG
WITH 1 TABLESPOON
OF BAKING SODA

HOLES

PURPOSE To determine why there are holes in bread slices.

MATERIALS

1 bowl, 1 qt (1 liter)
measuring cup (250 ml)
1 cup (250 ml) flour
measuring tablespoon (15 ml)
3 tablespoons (45 ml) sugar

1 package yeast, ¼ oz (7 g)
stirring spoon
1 bowl, 2 qt (2 liter)
1 paper towel

PROCEDURE

1. In a 1-quart (1-liter) bowl mix together 1 cup (250 ml) of flour, 3 tablespoons (45 ml) of sugar, 1 package of yeast, and 1 cup (250 ml) of warm water from the faucet. Stir.

2. Into the empty 2-quart (2-liter) bowl pour 3 cups (750 ml) of warm water from the faucet.

3. Set the small bowl with the flour mixture into the larger bowl of warm water.

4. Cover the top of the bowls with the paper towel.

5. Lift the paper towel every thirty minutes for four hours and observe the surface of the mixture in the bowl.

RESULTS A few bubbles appear on the surface of the mixture after thirty minutes. As time passes, more bubbles are seen and the surface of the mixture rises in the bowl.

WHY? Making bread involves a chemical reaction (the changing to new substances). One of the ingredients in making bread is a tiny, one-celled living fungus called yeast. This hungry fungus eats the sugar and changes it into carbon dioxide gas, alcohol, and energy. The bubbles observed in this experiment are carbon dioxide; they produce holes as they rise through the flour mixture. This same gas causes bread to rise during baking as the bubbles push the dough outward. Holes made by pockets of gas can be seen in slices of baked bread.

GLOB

PURPOSE To discover how a non-Newtonian fluid behaves.

MATERIALS

4-oz (120-ml) bottle of white
   school glue
1 pint (500 ml) jar
food coloring, any color
1 bowl, 2 qt (liter)
measuring cup (250 ml)

1 pint (500 ml) distilled water
1 teaspoon (5 ml) borax powder
   (found in the supermarket with
   laundry detergents)
measuring teaspoon (5 ml)
stirring spoon

PROCEDURE

1. Pour the glue into a pint (500 ml) jar.

2. Fill the empty glue bottle with distilled water and pour the water into the jar containing the glue. Add ten drops of food coloring and stir well.

3. Put 1 cup (250 ml) distilled water and 1 teaspoon (5 ml) borax powder into the bowl. Stir until the powder dissolves.

4. Slowly pour the colored glue into the bowl containing the borax. Stir as you pour.

5. Take the thick glob that forms out of the bowl. Knead the glob with your hands until it is smooth and dry.

6. Try these experiments with the glob:
   - Roll it into a ball and bounce it on a smooth surface.
   - Hold it in your hands and quickly pull the ends in opposite directions.
   - Hold it in your hands and slowly pull the ends in opposite directions.

RESULTS Kneading quickly dries the glob and results in a piece of soft pliable material that bounces slightly when dropped. It snaps if pulled quickly, but stretches if pulled slowly.

WHY? This most unusual material is an example of a non-Newtonian fluid. Fluids (anything that can flow) have a property called viscosity (the thickness of a fluid or its resistance to flowing). In the 1600s, Sir Isaac Newton stated that only a change in temperature could change the viscosity of a fluid. Fluids that change viscosity due to temperature changes are called Newtonian fluids. Non-Newtonian fluids' ability to flow, however, can also be changed by applying a force. Pushing or pulling on the piece of glob makes it thicker and less able to flow.

GREEN PENNIES

PURPOSE To give pennies a green coating.

MATERIALS paper towel
saucer
vinegar
3 to 5 pennies

PROCEDURE

1. Fold the paper towel in half; fold again to form a square.

2. Place the folded towel in the saucer.

3. Pour enough vinegar into the saucer to wet the towel.

4. Place the pennies on top of the wet paper towel.

5. Wait twenty-four hours.

RESULTS The tops of the pennies are green.

WHY? Vinegar's chemical name is acetic acid. The acetate part of the acid combines with the copper on the pennies to form copper acetate, the green coating you see on the pennies.

VINEGAR

PENNIES

SAUCER

FOLDED
WET PAPER TOWEL

Green Pennies

BREAKDOWN

PURPOSE To change hydrogen peroxide into water and oxygen with the aid of a potato.

MATERIALS hydrogen peroxide, household strength 3%
raw potato
5-oz (150-ml) paper cup

PROCEDURE

1. Fill the paper cup halfway with hydrogen peroxide.

2. Add a slice of raw potato to the cup.

3. Observe the results. Look specifically for bubbles of gas.

RESULTS Bubbles of gas are given off.

WHY? Raw potatoes contain the enzyme catalase. Enzymes are chemicals found in living cells. Their purpose is to speed up the breakdown of complex food chemicals into smaller, simpler, more usable parts. Catalase from the potato's cells causes the hydrogen peroxide to quickly break apart into water and oxygen gas.

Breakdown

STARCH I.D.

PURPOSE To determine how to test materials for the presence of starch.

MATERIALS ¼ teaspoon (1 ml) flour
measuring tablespoon (45 ml)
saucer
tincture of iodine

PROCEDURE

1. Place 1/4 teaspoon (1 ml) of flour in a saucer.

2. Add 3 tablespoons (45 ml) of water and stir.

3. Add three or four drops of the tincture of iodine.

RESULTS The combination of starch and iodine produces an intense blue-purple color.

WHY? Starch is a very large chemical molecule. It looks like a long, twisted chain with many branches sticking out. This long, twisted chain is thought to capture the iodine inside its spiral pattern. The spiral of starch with iodine caught on the inside produces the color.

MAGIC WRITING

PURPOSE To write a message that magically appears.

MATERIALS
soup bowl
cup (250 ml)
tincture of iodine
eyedropper

lemon
notebook
paper
art brush

PROCEDURE

1. Pour 1/2 cup (125 ml) water into a soup bowl.

2. Add ten drops of tincture of iodine to the water and stir.

3. Squeeze the juice of the lemon into the cup.

4. Cut a section from the notebook paper. The paper must fit inside the bowl.

5. Dip the art brush into the lemon juice and write a message on the piece of paper.

6. Allow the juice to dry on the paper.

7. Submerse the paper in the iodine solution in the bowl.

RESULTS The paper turns a blue-purple except where the message was written. The words are outlined by the dark background.

WHY? The starch in the paper combines with the iodine to form iodine-starch molecules. These molecules are blue-purple in color. Vitamin C combines with iodine to form a colorless molecule. The area covered with lemon juice remains unchanged because the paper is coated with vitamin C from the lemon.

Magic Writing

CURDS AND WHEY

PURPOSE To separate milk into its solid and liquid parts.

MATERIALS milk
small baby food jar
vinegar
measuring tablespoon (15 ml)

PROCEDURE

1. Fill the jar with fresh milk.

2. Add 2 tablespoons (30 ml) of vinegar and stir.

3. Allow the jar to sit for two to three minutes.

RESULTS The milk separates into two parts: a white solid and a clear liquid.

WHY? A colloid is a mixture of liquids and very tiny particles that are spread throughout the liquid. Milk is an example of a colloid. The solid particles in milk are evenly spread throughout the liquid. Vinegar causes the small undissolved particles to clump together, forming a solid called curd. The liquid portion is referred to as whey.

Curds and Whey

COOLER

PURPOSE To demonstrate that evaporation takes away heat.

MATERIALS clay flowerpot
bucket, large enough to hold the clay flowerpot
bowl, large enough to set the clay flowerpot in
clay, enough to plug the whole in the flower pot
table
2 thermometers
2 drinking glasses, large enough to hold a thermometer
electric fan

PROCEDURE

1. Place the clay flowerpot in a bucket of water and let it soak for one day.

2. Fill a bowl with water to a depth of about 1 in (2.5 cm) and set the bowl on a table.

3. Stand a thermometer in a glass and set the glass in the center of the bowl.

4. Turn the wet flowerpot upside down and stand it in the bowl so that it covers the glass and the thermometer. Put a clay plug in the hole in the flowerpot.

5. Stand a thermometer in a second glass, and set the glass on the table next to the bowl.

6. Record the reading on both thermometers.

7. Position a fan so that it blows equally on the flowerpot and on the glass standing on the table.

8. Record the reading on both thermometers every ten minutes for one hour. *Note:* Quickly replace the pot after each reading.

RESULTS The temperature under the pot is lower than the temperature outside the pot.

WHY? Evaporation occurs when a liquid absorbs enough heat energy to change from a liquid to a gas. As the water evaporates from the clay pot, it takes energy away; thus, the air underneath the pot is cooler than the air outside. Water from the bowl is soaked up by the pot, and so the evaporation and cooling process continues.

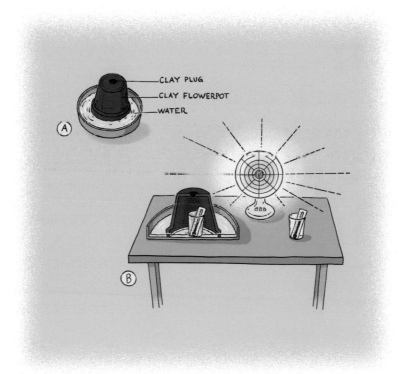

FROZEN ORANGE CUBES

PURPOSE To determine whether orange juice will freeze like water.

MATERIALS orange juice
water
ice tray
refrigerator

PROCEDURE

1. Fill half of the ice tray with orange juice.

2. Fill the remaining half of the ice tray with water.

3. Set the tray in the freezer overnight.

4. Remove the frozen cubes.

5. Carefully try to bite into a cube of orange juice and a cube of water.

RESULTS The liquid orange juice and water both change to solids. The frozen cube of orange juice is not as firm as the cube of ice. It is easy to eat the cube of orange juice.

WHY? The liquids both lost energy and changed from liquids to solids. The orange juice does not become as firm as the water because all the materials in the juice are not frozen. Many liquids freeze at a lower temperature than water does. Most of the frozen material in the juice is water. The juice cube is a combination of frozen and unfrozen material that makes it easy to eat.

Frozen Orange Cubes

CRYSTAL INK

PURPOSE To produce a message written with shiny crystals.

MATERIALS table salt
measuring teaspoon (5 ml)
measuring cup (250 ml)
stove with an oven
art brush
1 sheet black construction paper
Warning: Adult supervision is needed for use of the oven.

PROCEDURE

1. Add 3 teaspoons (15 ml) of salt to 1/4 cup (60 ml) water.

2. Ask an adult helper to warm the oven to 150°F (66°C).

3. Use an art brush to write a message on the black paper. Stir the salt solution with the brush before making each letter. It is important to do this in order to produce a clear message.

4. Have the adult helper turn the oven off and place the paper in the oven on top of the wire racks.

5. Allow the paper to heat for five minutes or until it dries.

RESULTS The message appears as white, shiny crystals on a black background.

WHY? The water evaporates, leaving dry salt crystals on the paper. Evaporation is the process by which a material changes from a liquid to a gas. Liquid molecules are in constant motion, moving at different speeds and in different directions. When the molecules reach the surface with enough speed, they break through and become gas molecules. Heating the paper speeds up the evaporation process.

FLUFFY AND WHITE

PURPOSE To observe the growth of fluffy white crystals.

MATERIALS 4 to 5 charcoal briquettes
2-qt (2-liter) glass bowl
cup
1 tablespoon (15 ml) household ammonia
2 tablespoons (30 ml) water
1 tablespoon (15 ml) table salt
2 tablespoons (30 ml) laundry bluing

PROCEDURE

1. Place the charcoal briquettes in the bowl.

2. In a cup, mix together the ammonia, water, table salt, and bluing.

3. Pour the liquid mixture over the charcoal.

4. Allow the bowl to sit undisturbed for seventy-two hours.

RESULTS White fluffy crystals form on top of the charcoal, and some climb up the sides of the bowl.

WHY? There are different kinds of chemicals dissolved in the water. As the water evaporates, a thin layer of crystals forms on the surface. These crystals are porous like a sponge, and the liquid below moves into the openings. Water again evaporates at the surface, leaving another layer of crystals. This continues, resulting in a buildup of fluffy white crystals.

Fluffy and White

ESCAPE

PURPOSE To demonstrate the removal of gas from a solution.

MATERIALS bottle of soda, 16 oz (480 ml)
balloon, 9 in (23 cm)
duct tape

PROCEDURE

Note: This experiment should be performed outdoors.

1. Remove the cap from a bottle of soda.

2. Stretch the mouth of a balloon over the mouth of the soda bottle.

3. Use a strip of duct tape to secure the mouth of the balloon to the bottle.

4. Hold your thumb over the mouth of the bottle and shake the bottle gently.

5. Set the bottle down.

6. Observe the balloon and the contents of the bottle.

RESULTS Bubbles form inside the bottle, and the balloon inflates.

WHY? A solution is the combination of a solute and a solvent. A solute is a material being dissolved and the solvent is a material doing the dissolving. In the soda, many solutes such as sugar, coloring, flavoring, and carbon dioxide are dissolved in the solvent, water. Large amounts of carbon dioxide are dissolved in the water by applying pressure. A "pop" is often heard when a bottle of soda is opened.

Opening the bottle releases the pressure, and undissolved gas at the top of the bottle escapes so quickly that a sound is heard. Shaking the bottle causes more gas to leave the liquid, forming bubbles that can be seen as they rise to the surface. The escaping carbon dioxide applies enough pressure on the walls of the balloon to inflate it.

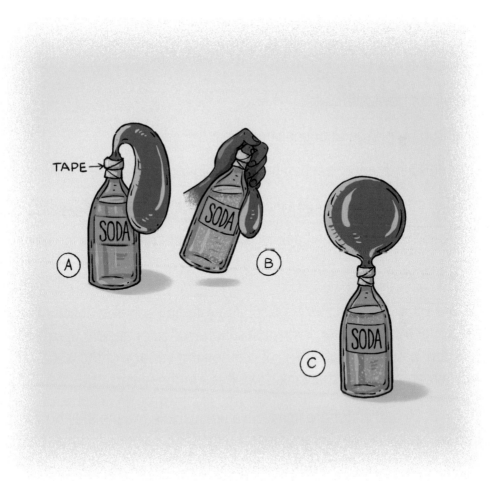

ERUPTING COLORS

PURPOSE To produce erupting color bubbles.

MATERIALS clear glass bowl, 2 qt (liter)
measuring tablespoon (15 ml)
liquid cooking oil
food coloring—red, blue, green
cup (250 ml)
fork

PROCEDURE

1. Fill the bowl with water.

2. Pour 1 tablespoon of cooking oil into the cup.

3. Add four drops of each of the food coloring colors.

4. Use the fork to beat the oil and colors until thoroughly mixed.

5. Pour the mixture of oil and food colors onto the water in the bowl.

6. Observe the surface and side of the bowl for five to ten minutes.

RESULTS Small pools of oil spotted with tiny spheres of color float on the surface of the water. Individual spheres of color appear to explode outward, producing flat circles of color on the surface of the water with streams of color that sink down through the water.

WHY? Oil and water are immiscible. Immiscible means they do not mix and will separate into layers. Because the food coloring is water based (it dissolves in water but not in oil), it remains in tiny spheres throughout the oil on the water's surface. The round, colored spheres sink through the oil layer and dissolve in the water layer below. At the moment the tiny drops of color touch the water, they quickly flatten on the surface, and long streamers of color begin their descent.

Tasty Solution

PURPOSE To determine the fastest way to dissolve candy.

MATERIALS 3 bite-sized pieces of soft candy

PROCEDURE

1. Place one of the candy pieces in your mouth. DO NOT chew, and DO NOT move your tongue around.

2. Record the time it takes for this candy piece to dissolve.

3. Place a second candy piece in your mouth. DO move the candy back and forth with your tongue, but DO NOT chew.

4. Record the time it takes to dissolve this candy piece.

5. Place the third piece of candy in your mouth. DO move the candy back and forth with your tongue as you chew.

6. Record the time it takes to dissolve this third piece of candy.

RESULTS Moving the candy around and chewing it decreases the time necessary for dissolving.

WHY? The candy dissolves in the saliva in your mouth to form a liquid solution. Solutions contain two parts, a solute and a solvent. The solvent is the saliva and the solute is the candy. The solute dissolves by spreading out evenly throughout the solvent. The candy can quickly dissolve when it is crushed by chewing and stirred by moving it around with the tongue.

Tasty Solution

RAINBOW EFFECT

PURPOSE To observe the separation of colors in ink.

MATERIALS coffee filter
paper clip
green and black water-soluble pens
saucer

PROCEDURE

1. Fold the coffee filter in half.

2. Fold it in half again.

3. Make a dark green mark about 1 in (2–3 cm) from the rounded edge of the folded filter.

4. Make a second mark with the black marker about 1 in (2–3 cm) from the rounded edge. The two marks are not to touch each other, but need to be on the same side.

5. Secure the edge of the filter with the paper clip so that a cone is formed.

6. Fill the saucer with water.

7. Place the rounded edge of the cone in the water.

8. Allow the paper to stand undisturbed for one hour.

RESULTS It takes about one hour for the colors to separate. A trail of blue, yellow, and red is seen from the black mark, and the green mark produces a trail of blue and yellow.

WHY? Black and green are combinations of other colors. As the water rises in the paper, the ink dissolves in it. Some of the colors rise to different heights, depending on the solubility of the chemicals producing the color. The more soluble chemicals move with the water to the top of the paper.

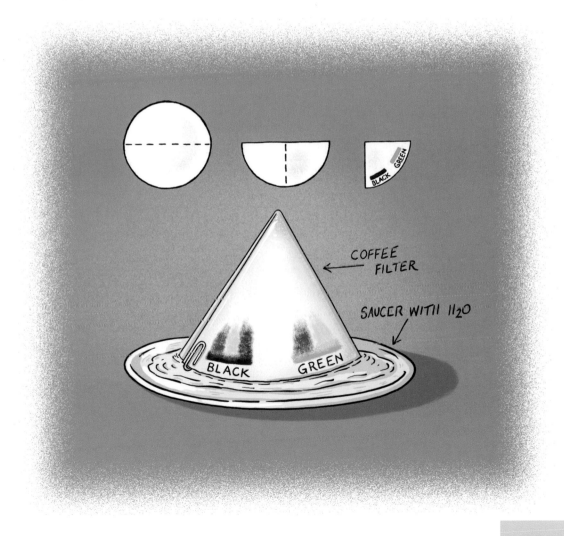

GLOSSARY

ABSORB To soak up or take in.

ADSORB To collect on a surface.

CATALASE An enzyme found in raw potato.

CHEMICAL REACTION The changing to a new substance.

COLLOID A mixture of liquids and very tiny particles that are spread throughout a liquid.

CURD The solid portion made when turning milk into cheese.

ENZYME A chemical found in living things that speeds up the breakdown of complex food chemicals into smaller, simpler more usable parts.

EVAPORATION The process by which a liquid absorbs enough heat to change into a gas.

FLUID Any substance that can flow.

MOLECULE The smallest particle of a substance; made of one or more atoms.

NEWTONIAN FLUIDS Fluids that change viscosity due to temperature changes.

NON-NEWTONIAN FLUIDS Fluids that are different from Newtonian fluids. Their flow is changed when a force is applied.

SOLUTE A material being dissolved.

SOLUTION A combination of a solute and a solvent.

SOLVENT A material doing the dissolving.

VISCOCITY The thickness of a fluid or its resistance to flowing.

WHEY The liquid portion left over when turning milk into cheese.

YEAST A one-celled living fungus.

American Association for the Advancement of Science (AAAS)
1200 New York Ave NW
Washington, DC 20005
(202) 326-6400
Website: http://www.aaas.org
The AAAS has been promoting the advancement of science for over 150 years. Take part in Family Science Days, learn about the latest discoveries through their daily Science Update, or see their choices for the best science books for kids.

American Chemical Society (ACS)
1155 Sixteenth Street NW
Washington, DC 20036
(800) 333-9511
Website: http://www.acs.org
The American Chemical Society has free educational resources, including experiments and games in their Adventures in Chemistry program; high school chemistry clubs; the Chemistry Olympiad competition for students; and Project SEED summer research programs. They educate the public during National Chemistry Week.

Chemical Institute of Canada
222 Queen Street, Suite 400
Ottawa, ON K1P 5V9
Canada
(888) 542-2242
Website: http://www.cheminst.ca
The Chemical Institute of Canada provides information about science fairs, scholarships, and the Canadian Chemistry Contest.

National Science Foundation (NSF)
4201 Wilson Boulevard
Arlington, VA 22230
(703) 292-5111
Website: http://www.nsf.gov
The NSF is dedicated to science, engineering, and education. Learn how to be a Citizen Scientist, read about the latest scientific discoveries, and find out about the newest innovations in technology.

The Society for Science and the Public
Student Science
1719 N Street NW
Washington, DC 20036
(800) 552-4412
Website: http://student.societyforscience.org
The Society for Science and the Public presents many science resources, such as science news for students, the latest updates on the Intel Science Talent Search and the Intel International Science and Engineering Fair, and information about cool jobs and doing science.

Websites

Because of the changing nature of internet links, Rosen Publishing has developed an online list of websites related to the subject of this book. This site is updated regularly. Please use this link to access the list:

http://www.rosenlinks.com/JVCW/chem

FOR FURTHER READING

Biskup, Agnieszka. *Super Cool Chemical Reaction Activities with Max Axiom* (Max Axiom Science and Engineering Activities). North Mankato, MN: Capstone Press, 2015.

Buczynski, Sandy. *Designing a Winning Science Fair Project* (Information Explorer Junior). Ann Arbor, MI: Cherry Lake Publishing, 2014.

Cobb, Vicki. *Science Experiments You Can Eat*. New York, NY: HarperCollins Publishers, 2016.

Heinecke, Liz Lee. *Outdoor Science Lab for Kids: 52 Family-Friendly Experiments for the Yard, Garden, Playground, and Park*. Beverly, MA: Quarry Books, 2016.

Henneberg, Susan. *Creating Science Fair Projects with Cool New Digital Tools* (Way Beyond PowerPoint: Making 21st Century Presentations). New York, NY: Rosen Central, 2014.

Mercer, Bobby. *Junk Drawer Chemistry: 50 Awesome Experiments that Don't Cost a Thing*. Chicago, IL: Chicago Review Press, 2015.

Miller, Rachel. *The 101 Coolest Simple Science Experiments: Awesome Things to Do with Your Parents, Babysitters, and Other Adults*. Salem, MA: Page Street Publishing Co., 2016.

Navarro, Paula. *Incredible Experiments with Chemical Reactions and Mixtures* (Magic Science). Hauppague, NY: Barron's Educational Series, 2014.

O'Quinn, Amy M. *Marie Curie for Kids: Her Life and Scientific Discoveries, With 21 Activities and Experiments*. Chicago, IL: Chicago Review Press, 2017.

Rompella, Natalie. *Experiments in Material and Matter with Toys and Everyday Stuff* (First Facts: Fun Science). North Mankato, MN: Capstone Press, 2016.

Royston, Angela. *Experiments with Water* (One-Stop Science). Mankato, MN: Smart Apple Media, 2016.

Thomas, Isabel. *Experiments with Materials* (Read and Experiment). Chicago, IL: Heinemann Raintree, 2016.

Wheeler-Toppen, Jodi. *Cool Chemistry Activities for Girls* (Girls Science Club). Mankato, MN: Capstone Press, 2012.

INDEX

A

acetate, 30
acetic acid, 30
air, cleaning of, 24–25
alcohol, 27

B

baking soda, 16, 19, 24, 25

C

carbon dioxide
    in bread making, 26–27
    creating, 18–19
    and salt, 14
    in volcanoes, 16
catalase, 32
    effect on hydrogen peroxide, 32
chemical reactions, 27
chemistry
    definition, 4
    fields of, 4
colloid, 38
colors, separating, 54–55
copper, 30
copper acetate, 30
crystals, 44–45, 46
curd, 38

E

effervescence, 14
energy, 27, 41, 42
enzymes, 32
    reaction to oxygen, 20
evaporation, 40–41, 44, 45

F

fluid, 29
    Newtonian, 29
    non-Newtonian, 28–29
freezing liquids, 42
fungus, 27

H

hydrogen peroxide, 32

I

immiscible, 50
iodine, 34, 36

M

matter, 4, 14

N

Newton, Isaac, 29
    non-Newtonian fluid, 28–29